HURRICANES and TORNADOES

Keith Greenberg

TWENTY-FIRST CENTURY BOOKS

A Division of Henry Holt and Company
New York

Twenty-First Century Books
A division of Henry Holt and Company, Inc.
115 West 18th Street
New York, New York 10011

Henry Holt® and colophon are trademarks of Henry Holt and
Company, Inc.
Publishers since 1866

©1994 by Blackbirch Graphics, Inc.
First Edition
5 4 3 2 1

Published in Canada by Fitzhenry & Whiteside Ltd.
195 Allstate Parkway, Markham, Ontario L3R 4T8

Printed in the United States of America

All editions are printed on acid-free paper ∞.

Created and produced in association with Blackbirch Graphics, Inc.

Library of Congress Cataloging-in-Publication Data

Greenberg, Keith. 1959–
     Hurricanes and tornadoes / Keith Greenberg. — 1st ed.
          p.   cm. — (When disaster strikes)
     Includes index.
     ISBN 0-8050-3095-6 (alk. paper)
     1. Storms—North America—Juvenile literature. 2. Natural disasters—North
America—Juvenile literature. 3. Hurricanes—North America—Juvenile literature.
4. Tornadoes—North America—Juvenile literature. 5. Cyclones—North
America—Juvenile literature. [1. Storms. 2. Hurricanes. 3. Tornadoes. 4.
Cyclones.] I. Title. II. Series.
     QC941.3.G74   1994
     363.3'492—dc20
                                                              93-38269
                                                              CIP
                                                              AC

Contents

Nature's Fury

Mary Ann had heard the storm warnings, but she did not leave.

After her ordeal was over, she would devote her energy to cautioning people not to make the same mistake that she had made—a mistake that had almost cost Mary Ann her life.

In 1969, Mary Ann was living in Mississippi, when the people in her apartment building received the bad news: Hurricane Camille was about to strike. Despite advice from officials and hurricane experts, the residents refused to evacuate to a safer area and instead threw a hurricane party.

By the time Mary Ann realized her mistake, it was too late. Strong winds had reached 234 miles (377 kilometers) an hour, and waves from

Opposite:
This aerial view, taken the day after Hurricane Camille hit Mississippi, shows the devastation that the storm caused.

the Gulf of Mexico washed over the beach and into her building. The windows creaked, then shattered. The water pushed her bed halfway up to the ceiling. Soon, the building was crumbling, and she was floating out the window.

In an effort to keep from drowning, Mary Ann latched onto a sofa pillow and tried to use it as a life preserver. But, she soon drifted into a snarl of wires and debris. In order to keep her head above water, she grabbed for anything she could reach—tree limbs, pieces of houses, furniture. But with the powerful winds, everything was blown out of her grasp.

Objects were whizzing past. Nails sticking out of broken pieces of lumber scratched Mary Ann, and her entire body was bloodied. After 12 hours of torture, she was finally saved— almost 5 miles (8 kilometers) from her home.

After three weeks in the hospital, Mary Ann had a totally new outlook. Never again would she take a hurricane lightly. Today, Mary Ann still lives in Mississippi, where she lectures people about the dangers of these storms and how to prepare for them.

Comparing Hurricanes and Tornadoes

Hurricanes and tornadoes are two of the most violent and devastating types of storms that occur, as Mary Ann and many other people have had the misfortune to experience. Aside from their very destructive characteristics, hurricanes and tornadoes share a few other similarities. Both of them depend on warm, moist air to start and both are accompanied by fierce winds, rain or hail, and low air pressure.

While hurricanes and tornadoes do have some things in common, they are two distinct types of storms. Hurricanes begin over water, and tornadoes start over land. A tornado has a shape like an upside-down cone, while a hurricane swirls around a calm center, or an eye, in a donutlike pattern. Although a hurricane is much larger and lasts longer, a tornado tends to be more treacherous and hits with less warning.

The spinning funnel cloud of a tornado can travel more than 300 miles (483 kilometers) an hour.

△ 7

When storm winds start gusting to 74 miles (119 kilometers) per hour, the storm is labeled a hurricane. Hurricanes create a rising wall of water that frequently washes onto beaches, piers, and private property. Called a storm surge, this water can climb as high as 25 feet (8 meters) above sea level. The storm surge is what is responsible for the greatest number of deaths during hurricanes, when many people drown in the roaring waters. In addition to ferocious winds and flooding, hurricanes bring heavy rains and, sometimes, tornadoes.

A tornado—also known as a twister—is distinguished by spinning, funnel-shaped clouds moving along the ground, and winds up to 310 miles (499 kilometers) per hour. Anything that stands in its path—trees, cars, buildings—is in danger of being completely destroyed.

The Impact of Hurricanes and Tornadoes

What makes hurricanes and tornadoes so frightening is their sudden and destructive nature. One day, people living in a community may have no greater worry than what to eat for dinner. The next day, the same people may be despairing over ravaged homes and dead or missing relatives and friends, all because of the fury of nature—a fury so mighty that the sturdiest buildings often offer little protection.

A hurricane also takes its toll in damage to property, crops, and land. Damage has often been in the billions of dollars—$4 billion for Hurricane Camille, $10 billion for Hurricane Gilbert in 1988, and $30 billion for Hurricane Andrew in 1992.

Hurricane Andrew swept through Florida in August 1992. It was the most violent hurricane to have hit the Sunshine State in sixty years.

△ 9

Opposite:
A tornado spun through Illinois in August 1990, and destroyed this Plainfield high school.

Many hazards accompany tornadoes—flash floods, lightning, and high winds, for example. As in the case of hurricanes, these hazards bring death and destruction with them. Flash floods, which are the number one weather-related killers in the United States, cause more than 200 casualties annually. Lightning is responsible for the deaths of between 75 and 100 Americans every year. Damaging straight-line winds, which can reach up to 140 miles (225 kilometers) per hour in a twister, and large pieces of hail, sometimes as big as grapefruits, also present serious dangers.

The sheer force of hurricanes and tornadoes is stunning. One day's released energy from a hurricane could supply the electrical needs of the United States for six months. Hurricane winds can produce waves as high as 50 to 60 feet (15 to 18 meters). During the few short minutes that a tornado usually lasts, tons of water can be pulled out of the atmosphere and into the raging funnel. With its furious winds, a tornado can tear a path more than 1 mile (2 kilometers) wide and 50 miles (80 kilometers) long. Once, for example, a tornado that ripped through the town of Broken Bow, Oklahoma, carried a motel sign a total of 30 miles (18 kilometers), before depositing it across the state line in Arkansas.

Knowledge Means Safety

As with any other type of disaster, education about hurricanes and tornadoes is the best form of self-defense against them.

Because hurricanes begin over water and then move from place to place over land, it is possible to track them before they reach land. Warnings can be received 12 to 24 hours ahead of time, and the approximate site where the impending storm will strike land is usually known as many as 8 to 16 hours before the hurricane hits. As it moves from place to place, a hurricane can travel the coastline of the eastern United States within a two-week period.

With the population rising in states where tornadoes are most common, the likelihood of twister damage is steadily increasing. Many new

KINDS OF HURRICANES

By international agreement, *tropical cyclone* is the term for all cyclones originating over tropical waters. Therefore, a storm that is called a hurricane in North America and the Caribbean is also called a tropical cyclone. Hurricanes go by a variety of names in different parts of the world. In Southeast Asia, a hurricane is labeled a typhoon; in the Philippines, a baguio; and in Australia, a willy-willy.

Regardless of what these storms are called—hurricanes, cyclones, typhoons, baguios, or willy-willies—they are all essentially the same type of storm. There is only one difference between them—the storm's direction of rotation. In the Northern Hemisphere, these tropical storms rotate in a counterclockwise direction. In the Southern Hemisphere, they rotate in a clockwise direction.

residents of places like Kansas and Oklahoma have never experienced tornadoes before, and are not aware of the proper ways to prepare for one. Mobile homes are particularly at risk, along with houses without basements. (Basements can be used as shelters from the whirlwinds.)

It may take years to rebuild homes, schools, and businesses damaged by hurricanes and tornadoes. Getting over the emotional damage—bad memories, nightmares, fears of going outside—can take even longer. There is nothing that anyone can do to stop a disaster from hitting. But physical and psychological injuries can be avoided if people receive the proper information about the nature of these storms and methods of preparing for them.

National Hurricane Center director Dr. Bob Sheets (standing right) checks the status of Hurricane Hugo in 1989, with the help of two other officials from the center. The National Hurricane Center, located in Coral Gables, Florida, was established to track hurricanes.

△ 13

Hurricanes

In the United States, hurricanes occur with greater frequency in the temperate southern zone near the Atlantic Ocean and the Gulf of Mexico than in other parts of the country.

In a typical year, more than 100 disturbances with the possibility of turning into hurricanes affect the Atlantic Ocean, the Gulf of Mexico, and the Caribbean Sea. Generally, only 10 of these become tropical storms, and only 6 of them become hurricanes. During a relatively calm year, between 50 and 100 people may be killed, and millions of dollars' worth of property destroyed. During a bad year, several hundred people may die, and the cost of the destruction can reach billions of dollars.

Opposite:
Winds from Hurricane Gilbert brought rushing water onto the island of Jamaica in 1988, damaging hundreds of thousands of homes.

How and When Hurricanes Start

Heat and moist air are the two ingredients essential for a hurricane to start and grow in size. In summer and early fall, large masses of air heat up over warm oceans, absorb moisture, and start spinning in a column formation. With the sea surface heated, water evaporates into the air, creating a moist atmosphere. When the warm, moist air rises, the surrounding air starts circulating around this column.

As the column climbs, condensation occurs. This is the process by which water vapor turns into droplets of water, and heat is released. The heat warms the column, and the water drops create clouds, which develop into rains and thunderstorms. As winds carrying the storm increase, so does the likelihood of a hurricane.

HOW A HURRICANE FORMS

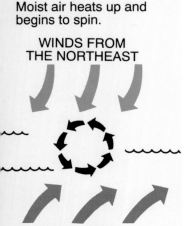

Moist air heats up and begins to spin.

WINDS FROM THE NORTHEAST

WINDS FROM THE SOUTHWEST
(Aerial View)

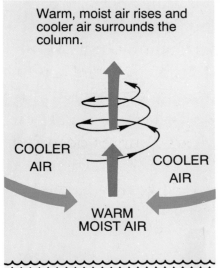

Warm, moist air rises and cooler air surrounds the column.

COOLER AIR

COOLER AIR

WARM MOIST AIR

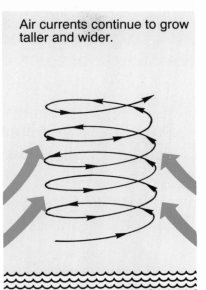

Air currents continue to grow taller and wider.

When winds reach 74 miles (119 kilometers) per hour, pressure falls swiftly in the eye of the storm. This area is deceptively calm. The most violent section of the disturbance is the region surrounding the eye—the eyewall. On land, the worst destruction occurs before and after the tranquil center passes through an area.

Hurricane Hazards

Wherever they strike, hurricanes are life-threatening. Debris caught up in the storm winds is as perilous as weapons fired in a war. When wind speed increases, the force of an object striking a person or another object rises as well. In winds of 25 miles (40 kilometers) per hour, a sheet of plywood is pushed with a force of 50 pounds (23 kilograms). In winds of up to 75 miles (121 kilometers) per hour, that force is 450 pounds (204 kilograms). A person hit by a projectile under these circumstances faces serious injury or death.

Water weighs 1,700 pounds per cubic yard (772 kilograms per cubic meter), making the storm surge dangerous. During hurricanes, it can rise to 25 feet (8 meters) high and 50 miles (80 kilometers) wide. Two deadly surges occurred in August 1893, in Charleston, South Carolina, and in September 1900, in Galveston, Texas, when thousands of people drowned.

△ 17

Typically, a hurricane also brings 6 to 12 inches (15 to 30 centimeters) of rain, spelling disaster for mountainous regions, where heavy rainfall often results in flash floods. After Hurricane Agnes in 1972, for example, rains at the end of the storm caused 118 deaths and $4.7 billion in property damage.

Major Hurricanes of the Twentieth Century

Hurricanes have been wreaking havoc for centuries. The first reports about their destructive nature were carried to Europe by Christopher Columbus. During his last voyage to the New World in 1502, he spotted hurricane conditions off what is now the Dominican Republic and reported this to the colonial governor. The governor, responsible for 30 ships, ignored the warning, while Columbus and his four-ship fleet sailed on to another port and waited for the storm to pass. Eventually, most of the vessels under the governor's control sank in the hurricane, but Columbus returned home safely.

During the twentieth century, careful records of hurricanes have been kept by the National Hurricane Center. The criteria used by the center to rank the severity of hurricanes include the category of storm (1 through 5, with 5 being the most severe), the death toll, and the amount of physical destruction.

Galveston, Texas: 1900

On September 2, 1900, a weather station in Cuba sent word that a hurricane was headed toward the island of Galveston, Texas. But residents did not seem too concerned. In the past, the city's sturdy seawalls had acted as protection from many storms. When rains began falling on September 8, and the storm surge increased, the most pressing worry seemed to be the safety of boats docked in the harbor.

This scene shows the devastating wreckage from the hurricane that hit Galveston, Texas, in 1900.

At midday, the waves smashing into the seawalls were larger than most citizens had ever seen. By 3:00 P.M., water started flooding the streets. Soon, all roads to the mainland were washed away, and residents were trapped.

Then at 7:22 P.M., a 20-foot (6-meter) wave rose from the ocean and crashed down on, among other places, the Old Women's Home, killing everybody inside instantly. Ships were swept into the city streets, smashing through buildings. Tiles flew from roofs, hitting those searching for safety, piercing their bodies and killing them. A railroad trestle dislodged and floated into a building, shattering it and leaving all 50 inhabitants dead. Graves were torn open and corpses drifted through the city streets. By midnight, waves were hitting with the force of 1 million (907,000 metric) tons. And by morning, when the storm finally cleared, 6,000 of Galveston's 25,000 citizens had perished.

Florida Hurricanes of the 1920s and 1930s

In the early part of the century, when many Americans began moving to the warm climates of Florida, a lack of knowledge about hurricanes often proved deadly. During a storm that hit the Miami area on September 18, 1926, several of the newer residents first evacuated their homes, then began heading back during the misleading eye of the storm, and were hit by winds of 138 miles (222 kilometers) per hour and tides more than 13 feet (4 meters) above normal. By the end of the storm, a total of 243 people were dead.

A 1926 hurricane caused vast destruction along this West Palm Beach, Florida, waterfront.

In September 1928, a similar situation occurred in the Lake Okeechobee area. This time, however, the death toll was more than seven times higher. Tides 10 feet (3 meters) above normal and winds of 160 miles (257 kilometers) per hour resulted in the deaths of 1,836 Floridians.

Just as this storm was beginning to fade from memory, a hurricane in the Florida Keys on Labor Day, September 2, 1935, brought winds of 200 miles (322 kilometers) per hour, tides 20 feet (6 meters) above average, and 408 fatalities. Low air pressure caused windows to burst out of houses, sealed glass jars to explode, and refrigerator doors to suddenly open.

By September 1, the U.S. Weather Bureau had warned residents of the southern Florida communities of Miami, Palm Beach, and the Keys to prepare for a dangerous hurricane.

With waves of more than 20 feet (6 meters) descending upon the Florida Keys, those who had not fled north were doomed. The lighthouse at Alligator Reef was destroyed, wooden buildings were toppled, and an 11-car train filled with passengers blew off the tracks and was tossed onto its side.

The storm lasted 36 hours. When it was over, one of the first rescue teams on the scene transmitted a very simple message: "Almost nothing man-made stands." Of the 750 people

The 1935 Florida hurricane winds were strong enough to hurl this train off the tracks and onto its side. Storm-bound passengers, shown waving to the airplane from which this picture was taken, could not be rescued for several hours.

who had remained on the three Florida Keys during the hurricane, more than half were dead or missing.

Hurricane Camille: 1969

Residents of Mississippi had already been through many hurricanes when the urgent warnings regarding Hurricane Camille were issued. On August 17, 1969, about 200,000 people evacuated the Gulf Coast on the day the storm was scheduled to hit, but others stayed behind, calmed by reports that the center of the hurricane would strike the Florida Panhandle, about 100 miles (161 kilometers) to the east. Some even gathered for "hurricane parties," expecting to watch the tempestuous winds and violent waves through picture windows. But their confidence proved disastrous. In one apartment complex near the shore, 23 revelers were killed.

In Mississippi, coastal skies turned dark gray, and then menacingly black. Several large ships were swept 7 miles (11 kilometers) inland before crashing into a motel. In the town of Holcomb Rock, the James River, normally 8 feet (2 meters) deep, reached almost 48 feet (15 meters) deep.

After passing through the Gulf Coast, Hurricane Camille then vented its fury on Virginia and West Virginia, causing landslides and 111 deaths. The day after the storm hit Mississippi, rescuers surveyed the aftermath—broken utility poles and pine trees scattered everywhere; three cargo ships on the beach; 30,000 damaged homes; 145 dead bodies.

Rubble is all that remains of this 32-unit apartment building in Gulf Park, Mississippi, that was struck by Hurricane Camille.

Hurricane Gilbert: 1988

American tourists go to beautiful places like Jamaica and Mexico's Yucatán Peninsula so that they can bask in the sun and forget about their worries. But in September 1988, most visitors experienced more trouble than many had ever known back home when Hurricane Gilbert struck the holiday spots, bringing with it a total of almost $10 billion in property damage and causing 318 deaths.

Although the hurricane was 500 miles (805 kilometers) wide, the eye of the storm was only 20 miles (32 kilometers) across. That meant that the calm at the center of the hurricane was particularly short-lived. The strong winds of the surrounding eyewall were traveling at 175 miles (282 kilometers) per hour.

On September 11, the tempest hit Haiti, then proceeded to the Dominican Republic. The next day, four-fifths of the 500,000 houses on the island of Jamaica were damaged, a quarter beyond repair. Brick walls crumbled, and entire trees were blown through the air. All telephone, radio, and satellite communication from the country was cut off, and 1,200 panicky tourists took shelter at the Wyndham Beach Hotel in Montego Bay. One tourist compared living through the hurricane with "being hit by an atom bomb."

But the worst was yet to come. The storm swept over the Cayman Islands and arrived on September 13 at the beachfront hotels of Cancún—in Mexico's popular Yucatán Penin-sula—with winds of 218 miles (351 kilometers) per hour and a storm surge of 20 feet (6 meters).

Next, Hurricane Gilbert entered the United States, sparking dozens of tornadoes in Texas. Perhaps the only bright moment came when post-hurricane rains brought much needed moisture to parched crops in the Southeast.

Residents try to salvage material from their house that was destroyed by Hurricane Gilbert as it barreled through Jamaica in September 1988.

Hurricane Hugo: 1989

When Hurricane Hugo struck South Carolina between September 16 and 22, 1989, it caused $6 billion in property damage. Even with the hurricane 300 miles (483 kilometers) away, high winds of 40 miles (64 kilometers) per hour were whipping through the state. Authorities ordered a large-scale evacuation in the regions around Charleston, Columbia, Florence, and Myrtle Beach.

As the storm intensified, Charleston Mayor Joseph P. Riley, Jr. realized the city was going to suffer a direct hit. From City Hall, he said, "All we can do now is pray, and hope that all the precautions we have taken will be sufficient."

Soon, electricity went out all over the city, gas lines exploded, and electrical transformers atop telephone poles blew out. The storm surge, driven by winds of up to 150 miles (241 kilometers) an hour, welled over Charleston's seawall and smashed into the downtown area. About 80 percent of the city's buildings were damaged, and half of City Hall's roof blown away.

Outside Charleston, things were just as bad. The tiny fishing village of McClellanville, located on an island just off the coast, was cut off from the mainland. All 600 residents took refuge in Lincoln High School. The building eventually filled with more than 6 feet (2 meters) of water.

Residents prepared as best they could in Charleston, South Carolina, before hurricane winds and water rushed through the region in September 1989.

Every fishing pier between Myrtle Beach and Isle of Palms—a distance of more than 100 miles (161 kilometers)—was wrecked. In Isle of Palms, 100 boats ended up on top of houses.

Hurricane Hugo continued north to Charlotte, North Carolina, advanced to Virginia, West Virginia, and Pennsylvania, and finally died out over Canada. Along the way, 504 people were killed.

△ 27

Hurricane Andrew: 1992

The all-time hurricane damage record was set in 1992 by Andrew's more than $30 billion assault on south Florida. About 250,000 people were left homeless, and 86,000 found themselves without jobs when the storm ended. "In two hours, I lost my house, my job, and my dog," said resident Jerry Beckham.

After hitting the Bahamas with winds of 120 miles (193 kilometers) per hour on August 23, Andrew picked up speed, striking southern Florida with gusts of 165 miles (265 kilometers) per hour the next day. Slicing through Miami in a path between 20 and 35 miles (32 and 56 kilometers) wide, Andrew demolished whole city blocks knocking out electricity, telephone service, drinking water, and sewage treatment.

Mariela Lewis, with her husband, Al Fishkin, and their nine-year-old daughter, Abigail, were among those who ignored warnings and stayed home. They stocked up on lots of canned goods, bottled water, and candles, while much of their community evacuated. In their one-story cement house, Lewis said they expected to experience "at most, just a few days' inconvenience."

When winds began whipping against their home, the family took refuge in the hall. When that area no longer seemed safe, they switched to the bedroom, sliding underneath the bed and propping the mattress up against the frame to shield themselves from flying debris.

Then, they heard a series of explosions. "We could see the hallway filling up," Lewis wrote, "and soon we were lying in water that wouldn't stop coming.... I could see the fear in my daughter's eyes; she understood that we could drown right here in the house. But how could I promise my child that we'd be okay, when I wasn't at all sure of that myself?"

In the Miami suburb of Naranja, several neighbors gathered together in a bathroom in an effort to protect themselves. Bruce Powers pressed himself against the door, listening to the

Southern Florida suffered extensive damage from Hurricane Andrew. Entire neighborhoods were leveled during this terrible storm.

△ **29**

HURRICANE CATEGORIES

A number of factors, such as wind and storm surge, are used to determine the destructive power of a hurricane. The National Oceanic and Atmospheric Administration (NOAA) uses the Saffir/Simpson Hurricane Scale, which assigns hurricanes to five categories.

Category One: Minimal hurricanes with winds of 75 to 95 miles (121 to 153 kilometers) per hour. The storm surge is 4 to 5 feet (1 to 1.5 meters). Shrubbery, trees, and mobile homes not attached to the ground can be damaged.

Category Two: Moderate hurricanes with winds of 96 to 110 miles (154 to 177 kilometers) per hour, and a storm surge of 6 to 8 feet (2 to 3 meters). Most mobile homes, roofs, and piers can be damaged.

Category Three: Extensive hurricanes with winds of 111 to 130 miles (179 to 209 kilometers) per hour, and a storm surge of 9 to 12 feet (3 to 4 meters). In addition to damaging small houses, mobile homes can be completely destroyed and coastal areas can be flooded.

Category Four: Extreme hurricanes with winds of 131 to 155 miles (211 to 249 kilometers) per hour, with a storm surge of 13 to 18 feet (4 to 5 meters). Buildings can be damaged, beaches eroded, and roofs destroyed. People living within 6 miles (10 kilometers) of the water may be in danger.

Category Five: Catastrophic hurricanes with winds of more than 155 miles (250 kilometers) per hour and a storm surge of more than 18 feet (5 meters). Most buildings are damaged, and many are destroyed. People living within 10 miles (16 kilometers) of the water may be in danger.

noises of things shattering outside, while water rose up to the medicine chest, and the bathtub was unhinged from its place. "I've never been so scared in my life," Powers's sister-in-law Karen Brocato remembered. "I hope I die if I'm ever that afraid again."

Disasters can bring out both the best and the worst in people. National Guard troops were sent to the area to keep law and order, and the same 14,000 soldiers also assisted the needy by setting up electrical generators, mobile kitchens, and tents.

Hurricane Andrew reached Louisiana on August 25. Although the wind had slowed somewhat to 140 miles (225 kilometers) per hour, the damage was still enormous. Between 25,000 and 30,000 people lost their homes, and half of the state's $400 million sugar crop was destroyed.

By August 26, the storm had moved on to Mississippi, where it died out.

The National Guard was not alone in their efforts to help victims. Donations of food and supplies poured into Florida communities from concerned people all over the country.

ANIMAL-RESCUE EFFORTS

Pets often end up being left behind when a family must quickly evacuate from an area facing a natural disaster. This was the case when Hurricane Andrew struck southern Florida in August 1992. Since evacuation shelters would not accept animals, many who were concerned for the welfare of their pets had to bring them along as they drove the clogged highways in search of safe havens. Others were forced to leave their animals behind with ample supply of food, hoping

This emergency clinic in Miami cared for hundreds of pets that were stranded or injured during Hurricane Andrew.

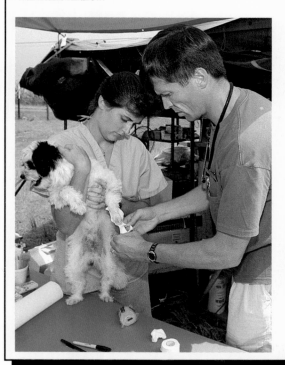

that their homes would remain intact and provide shelter for their pets.

Pet owners' worst fears were realized in Homestead, Florida, where 95 percent of the structures—including all 2,000 buildings at the U.S. Air Force base—were damaged. The dogs and cats that survived fled houses and apartment buildings in terror, only to be hit with flying debris. Elsewhere in the region, horses hurdled over upturned stable fences, and 2,000 primates escaped from Miami's Metrozoo.

Groups like the American Society for the Prevention of Cruelty to Animals (ASPCA) and the Humane Society of the United States (HSUS) were quick to ease the hardship. Tropical Park, a onetime racetrack, was converted into a clinic for wounded horses. Horses trapped up to their necks in mud were either rescued or, in cases where injuries were excessive, humanely destroyed. MASH (Mobile Army Surgical Hospital) units were set up to tend to other animals. Pet food, animal crates, and water were sent from other parts of the country. The Iams pet food company donated 44,000 pounds (19,976 kilograms) of food. Around the United States, people adopted pets that were cut off from their owners. During a two-week period, the MASH units housed more than 600 cats and dogs and provided veterinary attention to another 1,000 animals. A compound for larger animals tended to 110 horses, numerous cows, and a llama.

Other Notable Hurricanes

Hurricane Beulah struck the West Indies in September 1967, swept through Mexico's Yucatán Peninsula, and then sliced hard into Texas with winds of more than 160 miles (257 kilometers) per hour. Roofs were pried from houses, billboards were shredded, and 15 residents were killed. Then, 30 inches (76 centimeters) of rain pounded the state. As a result, people living in a region almost as big as the state of Ohio had to flee their homes, and 80 percent of the state's citrus crop was destroyed.

Hurricane Frederic, which swept over Alabama in 1979, stands as an example of how tragedies can be avoided if people pay attention to storm forecasts. On September 11, the hurricane appeared in the Gulf of Mexico, 350 miles (563 kilometers) southeast of Pensacola, Florida. At the National Hurricane Center, it was then determined that Hurricane Frederic would strike somewhere in the 290-mile (467-kilometer) area between Panama City, Florida, and New Orleans, Louisiana.

After some time, it became clear that the area along Alabama's Mobile Bay would become the storm's primary target. Using computer data, scientists studied Mobile Bay's features, then concluded that the storm surge near Gulf Shores, Alabama, would reach 12 feet (4 meters).

△ **33**

Using this information, officials evacuated 250,000 people on September 12. These residents were out of harm's way when Hurricane Frederic's winds of 145 miles (233 kilometers) per hour blustered over a stretch within 35 miles (56 kilometers) of Gulf Shores. As forecasted, the storm surge was 12 feet (4 meters). While the area sustained $2.3 billion in damage, only 7 people died.

Hurricane Gloria threatened to be the storm that would knock out New York City in 1985. After blowing across the outer banks of North Carolina in late September, it headed to the Northeast—a place generally immune to hurricanes—with winds of 130 miles (209 kilometers) per hour and 12-foot (4-meter) waves. New York officials warned residents to take precautions.

But Hurricane Gloria was not the terror that people expected. Although 10 people died in the storm, the tempest lost its energy minutes after hitting the bustling New York suburbs on Long Island. Still, authorities and broadcasters never regretted urging citizens to take the hurricane seriously. Bruce Schwoegler, the chief meteorologist at WBZ-TV in Boston, noted that the area suffered millions of dollars in lost business from people staying away. But he was quick to add, "It could have been millions of dollars, plus human lives, too."

HOW HURRICANES ARE NAMED

The naming of hurricanes has a meaningful purpose. It is possible that two hurricanes can be moving toward the same region at once. If each has a name, it makes distinguishing the two potential menaces easier.

Originally, hurricanes in the West Indies were named after the saint's day on which they occurred. Hurricane Santa Ana, for instance, struck Puerto Rico on Santa Ana—or Saint Ann's—Day in 1825.

At the end of the nineteenth century, Clement Wragge, an Australian meteorologist, started naming the disasters after women. The year's first storm would start with an *A*, the second with a *B*, and so forth. Most people liked this practice but, over the years, women's groups began to protest the custom of associating females with turmoil.

Finally, in 1979, men's and women's names were given alternately to hurricanes in the northern Pacific. A year later, the change carried over to storms in the Atlantic, Caribbean, and Gulf of Mexico. The first hurricane in North America given a male name was a weak storm—with winds slightly more than 75 miles (121 kilometers) per hour—called Hurricane Bob. It hit New England in August 1991, causing a small number of deaths and $1.5 billion in damage.

Since hurricanes affect countries other than the United States and are tracked by the weather services of many nations, hurricane names have an international flavor. They are selected by the World Meteorological Organization. The following is a list of the names chosen for 1994-1998 Atlantic storms.

1994	1995	1996	1997	1998
Alberto	Allison	Arthur	Ana	Alex
Beryl	Barry	Bertha	Bill	Bonnie
Chris	Chantal	Cesar	Claudette	Charley
Debby	Dean	Dolly	Danny	Danielle
Ernesto	Erin	Edouard	Erika	Earl
Florence	Felix	Fran	Fabian	Frances
Gordon	Gabrielle	Gustav	Grace	Georges
Helene	Humberto	Hortense	Henri	Hermine
Isaac	Iris	Isidore	Isabel	Ivan
Joyce	Jerry	Josephine	Juan	Jeanne
Keith	Karen	Kyle	Kate	Karl
Leslie	Luis	Lili	Larry	Lisa
Michael	Marilyn	Marco	Mindy	Mitch
Nadine	Noel	Nana	Nicholas	Nicole
Oscar	Opal	Omar	Odette	Otto
Patty	Pablo	Paloma	Peter	Paula
Rafael	Roxanne	Rene	Rose	Richard
Sandy	Sebastien	Sally	Sam	Shary
Tony	Tanya	Teddy	Teresa	Tomas
Valerie	Van	Vicky	Victor	Virginie
William	Wendy	Wilfred	Wanda	Walter

Tornadoes

When the skyscrapers, bridges, and elevated railway tracks of a city are seen from afar, it appears that people—with their unique ability to dream, plan, and build—have conquered nature. Perhaps it is only when disaster intrudes that nature reaffirms her authority, as when a 1931 Minnesota twister lifted an 83-ton (75-metric-ton) railroad car with 117 passengers and carried it in its powerful whirlwind for a total of 80 feet (24 meters)! This scenario is possible whenever a tornado hits, a situation that results in an average of 80 deaths and 1,500 injuries each year in the United States. Interestingly, most tornado deaths and injuries occur not from the storm itself, but from flying debris.

Opposite:
The sheer force and stunning beauty of a tornado are a startling combination to see, as this raging funnel carries a tall cloud of debris along with it.

Where and How Tornadoes Hit

Most tornadoes occur in the Midwest in an area known as "Tornado Alley," though twisters can strike anywhere in the United States. Tornado Alley begins in Texas, then runs up through Oklahoma, Kansas, Nebraska, and the Dakotas, ending in Canada. Winter tornadoes tend to hit the southern states, while the belt from Kansas to Kentucky is most vulnerable in the spring. The summer is a worrisome time for the Great Plains, Upper Midwest, and Canadian prairie provinces.

Tornadoes originate from severe thunderstorms. Of the 100,000 thunderstorms that the United States has annually, about 10,000 are severe. From these, 1,000 twisters develop—more than in any other country in the world.

The behavior of tornadoes can never be precisely predicted, but there are ways to identify them. Some are transparent at first, until a whirl of dust, soil, and debris is whipped up from the ground. The most visible type of twister is a big black cloud with a funnel running below it. The clearest sign of a tornado is the noise traveling miles ahead of the cloud—a blaring sound similar to that of a very loud train.

On the average, the deadly swirl of air moves southwest to northeast at a speed of about 35 miles (56 kilometers) per hour. Tornadoes

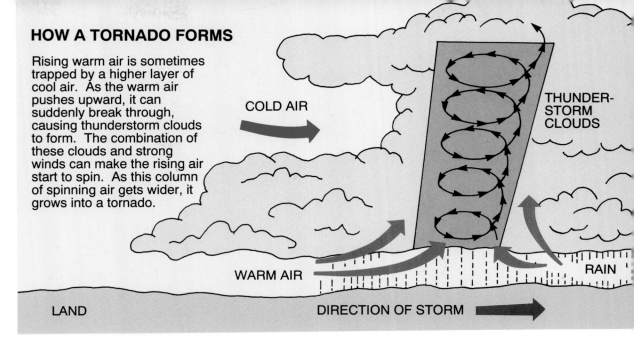

HOW A TORNADO FORMS

Rising warm air is sometimes trapped by a higher layer of cool air. As the warm air pushes upward, it can suddenly break through, causing thunderstorm clouds to form. The combination of these clouds and strong winds can make the rising air start to spin. As this column of spinning air gets wider, it grows into a tornado.

COLD AIR

THUNDER-STORM CLOUDS

WARM AIR

RAIN

LAND

DIRECTION OF STORM

don't often strike the same spot twice; however, some areas have repeatedly suffered tornado damage. For example, Oklahoma City, Oklahoma, was hit more than 25 times during the twentieth century, and Baldwin, Mississippi, was struck twice within 25 minutes on March 16, 1942. Codell, Kansas, was battered by tornadoes three years in a row—1916, 1917, and 1918—all on May 20.

The Life of a Tornado

A tornado often arrives with a tropical storm or while a hurricane is over land, traveling to the right and ahead of the storm center when it leaves the sea.

Weak tornadoes forming over warm water are called waterspouts. These occur most frequently along the Gulf Coast and southeastern states. On the West Coast, waterspouts develop with cold storms in late fall or winter. Water, air, and ocean spray are all absorbed into the rotating coils as they journey over the sea. When waterspouts move onto land, their intensity then increases, and they become full-blown twisters.

Tornadoes generally last less than twenty minutes, although some have not been so short-lived. As they begin to weaken, the funnel cloud starts to become ropelike, winding from side to side and scattering a haze of debris.

Twentieth-Century Tornadoes

The National Severe Storms Forecast Center in Kansas City, Missouri, constantly monitors the weather, watching for signs of tornadoes. The center also has records of the many tornadoes that have hit the United States and Canada.

Tristate Twister: 1925

The most harmful individual tornado ever to strike the United States occurred on March 18, 1925. It is referred to as the Tristate Twister because it hit Missouri, Illinois, and Indiana. The absence of a black funnel lulled residents into believing that the twister would not be destructive. Also, instead of rotating in different directions, the tempest moved in a straight line, faster than any other tornado ever recorded.

When the twister touched down at 1:00 P.M. in Annapolis, Missouri, it wiped out 90 percent of the town's buildings before continuing on and leveling every structure in Gorham, Illinois, and 40 percent of the town of Murphysboro. In East Frankfort, Illinois, 64 homes were ruined, timber was speared through a steel railroad car, and 16 students were blown out of their chairs at school and dropped—unharmed—450 feet (137 meters) away. In Indiana, 90 percent of the village of Parrish was wrecked, and 25 percent of the buildings in the town of Princeton were demolished.

This 1925 photograph shows a view of Griffin, Indiana, after the Tristate Twister ripped through the town.

In fewer than four hours—a long time for one tornado—219 miles (352 kilometers) of America's heartland had been shredded, and 689 lives had been lost.

Southern Invasion: 1936

"200-Mile-An Hour Death...Fiercer Than Fire, Swifter Than Flood, Tornado Hits Dixie."

This was the headline a magazine used to describe the severe tornadoes that struck six southern states on April 5 and 6, 1936. The tornadoes plowed through the states of Georgia, Mississippi, Tennessee, Alabama, Arkansas, and South Carolina.

Tupelo, Mississippi, was one of the first cities to experience the onslaught and one of the two

FUJITA SCALE FOR DAMAGING WINDS

The Fujita Scale for Damaging Winds measures a tornado's intensity. It was named for Professor Tetsuya T. Fujita who developed the scale in 1971. The Fujita Scale places twisters in the following categories:

Scale	Wind Speeds in Miles Per Hour	Wind Speeds in Kilometers Per Hour	Damage
0	40–72	64–116	Light
1	73–112	117–180	Moderate
2	113–157	182–253	Considerable
3	158–206	254–331	Severe
4	207–260	333–418	Devastating
5	261–318	420–512	Incredible

Source: American Red Cross

Workers clear away the ruins of the City Hall building in Gainesville, Georgia, after a 1936 twister destroyed the building.

hardest hit. With a terrifying noise, the first tornado ripped trees from the earth, destroyed buildings, killed 216 people, and left.

With nowhere safe to run, those caught in the path of the tornado were forced to improvise. One man actually pushed his family to safety through an open manhole cover.

With gas lines cut, fires broke out in several places. When firefighters arrived to extinguish the blazes, however, many of the hydrants were buried under large piles of rubble. Fortunately, the rain that followed the tornado helped douse the flames.

The next day, two other twisters, which were part of the April 5 outbreak, struck Gainesville,

Georgia. Fourteen city blocks were destroyed. Much of the small city's business district was wiped out, and 203 people were killed.

William Porter of Gordo, Alabama, was luckier than most in his situation. The 67-year-old was sick in bed when he heard a roar. The noise became louder and louder, until the whole house shook. Debris flew everywhere, and the roof was pulled off the building, but Mr. Porter remained in his bed, watching with amazement.

In addition to the 419 people who died in Tupelo and Gainesville, 2,000 others received injuries. The property damage was listed at $25 million, a high figure for the time.

Palm Sunday Tornadoes: 1965

On April 11, 1965, a mass of cool, dry air moving down quickly from western Canada met with a blend of warm, moist air blowing up from the Gulf of Mexico. This clash first caused storms over Texas and Oklahoma. Aided by a strong jet stream—a high-altitude air current—the storms moved northeast, and turned into twisters over the central United States.

A total of 35 tornadoes and 50 thunderstorms raged through parts of Iowa, Wisconsin, Illinois, Indiana, Ohio, and Michigan.

This collection of disturbances started with a thunderstorm south of Dubuque, Iowa. At about

1:20 P.M., the first funnel was reported. Within a half hour, another six would be seen in Iowa, Wisconsin, and Illinois.

In Crystal Lake, Illinois, insurance salesman Charles Swanson was pulled out of the shower as he readied himself for a party. "The next thing I knew, I was sliding out into the street with no clothes on," he said. "I got up and there was no house left."

In the small town of Russiaville, Indiana, all 1,200 residents suffered as every single building was damaged. Outside of Cleveland, Ohio, 17-year-old Dan Avins was sleeping soundly when the twister hit his house and knocked him—still safely in bed—35 feet (11 meters) into the yard.

In all, 242 people perished, but the torment continued. Rains that followed the tornadoes flooded 18,000 people out of their homes in Minnesota and killed 12 more.

13-State Terror: 1974

It seemed that no place in North America was safe from disaster. Within a period of 18 hours on April 3 and 4, 1974, a series of 148 tornadoes tore through the continent, from southern Canada all the way to Georgia. These were not isolated twisters, but an entire tornado system that whirled through 13 states. The vicious funnels, traveling at speeds between 200 and

300 miles (322 and 483 kilometers) per hour killed more than 300 people, injured 1,200 others, and caused a staggering $1 billion in property damage.

The tornadoes that ripped through these states also left behind bizarre tales to be told to future generations. In Stringtown, Indiana, for example, the Church of the Nazarene was almost completely destroyed—but the figures in the building's Nativity scene remained kneeling in place, untouched. In Jasper, Alabama, a radio reporter who was trying to gather details about the crisis explained to listeners, "We can't talk to the police department...it just blew away." In Xenia, Ohio, the town hardest hit by the tempest, a tractor-trailer truck was propelled off the ground, pushed through the air, and dropped—perfectly balanced—on top of a bowling alley.

The twister wiped out 6 of Xenia's 12 schools, 5 of its 7 supermarkets, and hundreds of homes. About 1,000 of the town's 25,000 residents were injured, and 30 were killed, as the tornado swept away school buses and turned over 30 cars of a freight train. "We had about 30 seconds warning before it hit," Gary Heflin, a grocery-store manager, remembered. "All you could hear was the wind, the crashes and the people praying."

This house in Xenia, Ohio, lost one whole side during a tornado in 1974, yet the furniture and the pictures on the wall look untouched.

Virginia Twister: 1993

When a tornado traveling 210 miles (338 kilometers) per hour touched down in Petersburg, Virginia, at 1:30 P.M. on Friday, August 6, 1993, everyone was shocked. Tornadoes rarely hit Virginia, and the state had not experienced such a deadly twister since 1959, when 10 people died in an Albemarle County tornado.

As the tornado moved along, its high winds diminished to 125 miles (201 kilometers) per hour, and it slammed into the Wal-Mart department store inside a Colonial Heights mall. The store was heavily damaged, 4 people were killed, and 119 others were injured.

No deaths occurred in Petersburg, but more than 30 people were hurt, and the city's historic Old Towne district was virtually destroyed.

△ **47**

Preparation and Protection

As the towns and cities of North America grow, so do the problems associated with hurricanes and tornadoes. Once tranquil prairies are now busy suburbs, cluttered with new townhouses that are flimsy enough to come crashing down in the event of a tornado. More and more people have retired to beachfront communities, where hurricanes are likely to hit. In addition, during the height of the vacation season, the number of people in resort towns like Ocean City, Maryland, Gulf Shores, Alabama, and Padre Island, Texas, increases between 10 and 100 times, making evacuation very difficult. To help

Opposite:
The National Center for Atmospheric Research in Boulder, Colorado, uses this Doppler radar unit to collect and measure wind speed and precipitation data.

communities survive these storms, agencies have been set up to keep track of weather disturbances both within the United States and outside the country, and sophisticated equipment has been developed.

Tracking the Storms

Satellites operated by the National Oceanic and Atmospheric Administration are used to monitor disturbances all over the world 24 hours a day. The National Hurricane Center tracks hurricanes, and the National Severe Storm Forecast Center is on the lookout for tornadoes.

Hurricane prediction in the early days had been based solely on surface reports from land stations or ships. Then, in the 1940s, aircraft began to be used to monitor hurricanes. Airplanes are still used, once satellites provide meteorologists with information about a hurricane that is likely to strike. The U.S. Air Force then sends out its hurricane trackers, which fly directly into the storm to determine the location of the hurricane's eye and to measure its winds and pressure fields.

The launching of the first weather satellite in 1960 represented the greatest advance in the early detection of hurricanes. By studying satellite photographs, National Hurricane Center scientists can monitor storms long before they ever turn into hurricanes.

Tornadoes are tracked by four means: surface weather observations, radiosonde balloons, radar, and satellite information. Because tornadoes are small, airplanes are not used; there is no equipment available that can see a tornado directly.

This satellite view of Hurricane Hugo shows the eye of the storm, where temperatures are the highest, in red. These pictures help meteorologists track where a hurricane is heading.

Surface weather observations—information about pressure, temperature, dew point, and other atmospheric conditions—are obtained from about 800 weather stations across the United States. Photographs from weather satellites are valuable in tracking tornadoes because they show where the clouds are. Doppler radar is a kind of radar that helps scientists learn about the speed and direction of the winds during storms. It also shows where precipitation is and the velocity of the precipitation, which enables meteorologists to determine the path a tornado will take.

Radiosonde balloons, which are sent up about 300 miles (483 kilometers) apart twice daily in 80 areas of the United States, send back

This Doppler radar unit (top) at the Denver, Colorado, airport is protected from strong winds by a globelike covering that allows the radar waves to pass through. Above is an interior view of the radar dish itself.

information to meteorologists via a tiny radio transmitter. The radiosonde balloons help in tornado detection by providing information about the make-up of the atmosphere—such as wind, moisture, air temperature, and pressure.

Be Informed and Heed the Warnings

Technology has been a boon to society when it comes to predicting and tracking hurricanes, and locating tornadoes. Even so, residents of a community have a responsibility to learn about these disasters, listen to weather forecasts, and heed the advice of the experts, in order to protect themselves.

Even if a hurricane or tornado rarely strikes your region, you should know the area's risk for such storms. What is the history of hurricanes and tornadoes in your town or city? Which areas are most likely to flood during a hurricane? To get answers to these and other questions, you can call your local chapter of the American Red Cross. You should also familiarize yourself with the warning signs of hurricanes and tornadoes.

Hurricanes are characterized by violent winds and, if they are located near shore, abnormally large waves.

A tornado's tell-tale signs include a dark, greenish sky, large hail, and a loud roar not unlike that of a freight train. Some tornadoes look like corkscrew-shaped clouds hovering above the ground, with debris swirling below. Others are hidden by rain or clouds and may come upon an area suddenly.

To prevent tragedy, authorities issue watches and warnings for hurricanes and tornadoes. A watch means that conditions are such that a hurricane or tornado could form. A warning means a hurricane or twister has been sighted.

Anticipating a Hurricane

When the National Weather Service issues a hurricane watch, residents should proceed as follows:

- Listen to the radio or watch the news on television for further instructions.
- Gather materials to board up buildings.

△ **53**

Residents of Miami, Florida, prepare for Hurricane Andrew by boarding up windows in 1992.

- Bring bicycles, lawn chairs, and any other objects that could blow away, indoors.
- Collect water in bathtubs, buckets, or other large containers.
- Make sure there are fresh batteries on hand for radios and flashlights.
- Fill up the car with gasoline.
- Determine a meeting spot in the event that any family members are separated during the storm.
- Be ready to evacuate if told to do so.

Anticipating a Tornado

The National Weather Service uses radar and eyewitness accounts to issue tornado watches and warnings, which are then broadcast over local television and radio stations. After learning of a tornado watch, residents should listen for further information and remain alert to any changing weather conditions.

After hearing a tornado warning—or noticing signs of a twister—you should immediately take shelter. All advance information regarding this threat is useless if you don't find safety.

Weathering the Storms

Once a hurricane or a tornado hits, what do you do? This is a question that everyone must think about before a disaster occurs.

Hurricane Guidelines

In the case of a hurricane, people must consider how they will evacuate if advised to do so. Those living in mobile homes, high-rise buildings, or in any type of structure along the coast, on an off-shore island, near a river, or in an area that frequently floods, are most likely to be told to evacuate. An evacuation warning should not be taken lightly, and every effort should be made to leave the area as quickly as possible. Homes of friends and relatives in a safer region and inland hotels or motels are the best choices for riding out the storm. Hurricane shelters are available for people with no other options, but these can be crowded. It is best to leave early for your final destination, before roads become congested, or bridges and highways flood. Because certain roads may be closed, people should keep a special "evacuation map," listing several alternate routes out of the area.

If the hurricane is not severe enough to warrant evacuation, the following steps should be taken:

- Stay inside—away from windows. To guard against winds, secure doors leading outside, and keep all interior doors closed.
- Go to the lowest floor in the building. Areas around stairs or elevator shafts tend to be the strongest places.
- Lie on the floor, under tables or other sturdy furniture.
- Continue to stay inside until otherwise advised, even when the skies are clear. You may be in the eye of the storm.

Tornado Guidelines

In anticipation of a tornado that may someday touch down in your neighborhood, you need to think about where in your house or apartment building you could take cover. A tornado strikes suddenly, so evacuation is not an option. As soon as you hear a tornado warning, you must act:

- Immediately seek shelter. A basement is the best place to go—make sure a section of your cellar is clear enough to serve as a retreat. If there is no basement, go to the lowest floor and into a bathroom, closet, or hallway in the center of the building.
- Stay away from windows.
- Protect your head.
- Leave a mobile home for a secure building. If there is no such structure nearby, lie flat in a ditch or low-lying area, using your hands to protect your head. (Be aware, however, that flash floods can accompany tornadoes.)

After the Storm

The end of the storm does not mean the end of problems for individuals, the community, the state, or even the nation. People who have lost their homes, or whose homes were seriously damaged, must find places to live. Relatives and friends often take them in. And sometimes disaster-relief funds are used to provide temporary shelter, as was the case with Hurricane Andrew.

People who are lucky enough to find their homes standing after a hurricane or tornado often need to make costly repairs. The communities in which they live may be without power for a time, and stores destroyed or damaged by the storm can no longer serve people's needs. With downed power lines, debris-strewn streets, trees whose limbs are in danger of falling, and possible looting, neighborhoods may not be safe. Communications may be cut off, and hospitals may be filled to capacity with the many injured.

Rebuilding areas that have been destroyed by hurricanes and tornadoes costs money—money that small towns, cities, and even states may not have. The federal government must then step in to provide financial aid. Where does this money come from? The taxpayers. Everyone, whether directly involved in the storm or not, is thus affected. Concerned citizens across the

An O'Fallon, Missouri, resident searches his house for any remaining belongings after a tornado destroyed 64 homes in 1988.

PLANNING A FAMILY SAFETY KIT

In the event that a natural disaster strikes your home, it is important to have a disaster kit to use until help can arrive. The American Red Cross recommends that these items be kept in a plastic garbage can, for no longer than six months. This container should be easily movable and may also be used later to save water. Among the articles the Red Cross suggests for the kit are:

- Canned food: Fish, meats, poultry, fruits, vegetables, soups, juices.
- First-aid kit, including bandages, sterile gauze pads, adhesive tape, scissors, tweezers, a needle, a safety-razor blade, regular soap, moistened towelettes, antiseptic spray, and matches.

- A three-day supply of bottled water (one gallon [4 liters] per person, per day).
- One change of clothing and footwear per person.
- One heavy blanket or sleeping bag per person.
- One can opener that does not require electricity to operate.
- Flashlight.
- Portable radio for monitoring news about the disaster.
- Extra batteries.
- Fire extinguisher.
- Essential medications.
- Any special items required by infants, the elderly, or disabled family members.

nation also try to pitch in, donating both time and money. Organizations such as the Red Cross, civic organizations, church groups, and private individuals are there to help.

While hurricanes and tornadoes bring a host of problems, they also bring an awareness to people—an awareness that should help them to be as prepared as possible for any future storm. Being prepared and knowing that people are genuinely concerned and willing to help in the face of disaster should help to lessen people's fears about nature's fury.

Glossary

condensation The process by which water vapor turns into droplets of water, and heat is released.

eye of a hurricane The deceptively calm center of a storm.

eyewall The most violent part of a hurricane, which surrounds the eye.

hurricane A tropical storm that is moving counterclockwise with winds of 74 miles (119 kilometers) per hour or greater.

hurricane trackers Aircraft designed to fly into hurricanes in order to monitor conditions.

jet stream A high-altitude air current.

meteorologist A scientist who specializes in analyzing weather data.

storm surge A rising wall of seawater created during a hurricane, which often washes onto beaches and may drown residents.

storm warning An official alert that a hurricane or a tornado has been sighted.

storm watch An official alert that a hurricane or a tornado may occur.

tornado A spinning, funnel-shaped cloud, which picks up debris and unleashes winds that can be more than 300 miles (483 kilometers) per hour.

tropical cyclone The term universally used to describe storms occurring over tropical waters whose winds are 74 miles (119 kilometers) per hour or greater, and are moving counter-clockwise; in North America and the Caribbean, a hurricane.

tropical storm A storm with winds of 39 to 73 miles (63 to 117 kilometers) per hour.

typhoon A hurricane-like storm that occurs in Southeast Asia.

waterspout A weak tornado forming over warm water.

Further Reading

Archer, Jules. *Hurricane!* New York: Macmillan, 1991.

_____. *Tornado!* New York: Macmillan, 1991.

Fradin, Dennis Brindell. *Hurricanes.* Chicago, IL: Childrens Press, 1982.

_____. *Tornadoes.* Chicago, IL: Childrens Press, 1982.

Lampton, Christopher. *Hurricane.* Brookfield, CT: Millbrook Press, 1991.

_____. *Tornado.* Brookfield, CT: Millbrook Press, 1991.

Twist, Clint. *Hurricanes & Storms.* New York: Macmillan, 1992.

HAVE YOU EVER FACED A DISASTER?

If you have ever had to be brave enough to face a hurricane or tornado, you probably have a few exciting stories to tell! Twenty-First Century Books invites you to write us a letter and share your experiences. The letter can describe any aspect of your true story—how you felt during the disaster; what happened to you, your family, or other people in your area; or how the disaster changed your life. Please send your letter to Disaster Editor, TFCB, 115 West 18th Street, New York, NY 10011. We look forward to hearing from you!

Source Notes

American Red Cross. *Family Survival Guide,* 1990.

Barneveld, Ruth Ehlert, and Barbara Hanson Pierce. "A Tornado Crushed My Life," *Redbook,* August 1986.

Bevan, Laura. "Struggle and Triumph in Andrew's Wake," *WSUS News,* Winter 1993.

"First the Wind, Then the Waters," *Newsweek,* April 26, 1965.

"The Funnels of Fury," *Newsweek,* April 15, 1974.

"Hurricane Beulah, One of the Big Ones," *U.S. News and World Report,* October 2, 1967.

Lewis, Mariela. "We Survived the Storm," *Ladies Home Journal,* December 1992.

"Man Vs. Nature: Still a Losing Fight," *U.S. News and World Report,* April 26, 1965.

Martz, Larry; Nonny Abbott; and Erik Colonius. "Gilbert's Havoc," *Newsweek,* September 26, 1988.

Shapiro, Walter. "Sic Transit Gloria," *Newsweek,* October 7, 1985.

Stevens, William. "3 Disturbances Become a Big Storm," *The New York Times,* March 14, 1993.

"Tornadoes: Ill Winds Blow a Few Southern States No Good," *Newsweek,* April 11, 1936.

"200 Mile An Hour Death," *Literary Digest,* April 18, 1936.

U.S. Department of Commerce. *Hurricane! A Familiarization Booklet,* April 1993.

_____. *Tornadoes...Nature's Most Violent Storms,* September 1992.

_____. *Watch Out, Storms Ahead,* March 1984.

Index

Acknowledgements and Photo Credits

Cover: ©Sheila Beougher/Liaison International; p. 4: Bettmann Newsphotos; pp. 7, 23: National Weather Service; p. 9: ©Susan Greenwood/Gamma Liaison; pp. 11, 13, 58: Wide World Photos; p. 14: Gamma Liaison; p. 19: The Bettmann Archive; pp. 20, 46: UPI/Bettmann Newsphotos; pp. 22, 41, 43: UPI/Bettmann; p. 25: Reuters/Bettmann; p. 27: ©Jeff Amberg/Gamma Liaison; p. 29: B. Wisser/Liaison USA; pp. 31, 32: ©John Berry/Gamma Liaison Network; p. 36: ©1989 C. Doswell; p. 48: Charles Knight/National Center for Atmospheric Research; p. 51: National Oceanic and Atmospheric Administration; p. 52: National Center for Atmospheric Research (top & bottom); p. 54: T. Savino/Liaison USA.

Art by Blackbirch Graphics, Inc.